PRAISE. OR
THE *Chronic* ENTREPRENEUR

Essential reading for anyone with a chronic condition who is seeking the freedom and joy of an entrepreneurial life.

This friendly, practical guide focuses on what you CAN do and is an exciting invitation to build a profitable and flexible business, so you can live well and thrive.

Be inspired by Lisa's own story – and those of other chronic entrepreneurs – who have proven there are alternatives to doing draining, soulless jobs that do not work around your condition.

Instead, follow the step-by-step instructions for finding your perfect business venture, putting the practicalities into place and working to the beat of your own drum – prioritising happiness and self-care in the process.

Uplifting. Empowering. Transformative.

Michelle Ewen, Write On Time
Chronic Entrepreneur managing Panic Disorder

THE
Chronic
ENTREPRENEUR

How to set up and run your own
business alongside a chronic condition

Lisa Porto

First published in 2022 by Fuzzy Flamingo
Copyright © Lisa Porto 2022

Lisa Porto has asserted her right to be identified as the author of this
Work in accordance with the Copyright, Designs and Patents Act 1988.

ISBN: 978-1-7397850-1-7

Cover photo © Becky Wright Brand Photography
www.beckywrightbrandphotography.com

Editing and design by Fuzzy Flamingo
www.fuzzyflamingo.co.uk

A catalogue for this book is available from the British Library.

To those who believed in me from the very beginning, and stuck with me (you know who you are), thank you. I wouldn't be where I am today without your ongoing love and support, and without that, this book wouldn't have been possible.

Contents

Foreword

Being an entrepreneur is hard. I know you may have wanted a more uplifting and motivating start to this wonderful book but let's start with the reality of juggling it all, whilst creating a wonderful life for yourself. At times it's hard, but – and this is one huge but – once you get yourself a system together (and most importantly a system that works with you), being an entrepreneur is the most exhilarating and rewarding life you can ever imagine.

As a person with ADHD I massively value the way this book is formatted and being able to refer back to the areas that I need with ease.

This book is your one-stop shop to building your business, in a realistic way, that works around all of your personal challenges. I wish I had had this book when I first started out in business.

Holly Matthews
Self development coach
and founder of The Happy Me Project

Introduction

Who is the book for?

If you have a chronic condition and want to set up your own business to give yourself more flexibility to improve your health, then this book is for you.

Having a chronic condition can make being employed tricky:

- Commutes to and from work can be stressful and exhausting (that's without the actual 'work' in between).
- Little or no flexibility in working hours can make it difficult on these 'bad' days.
- Time off sick or to attend medical appointments can sometimes be difficult for employers to understand.
- Employers' and colleagues' lack of understanding or incorrect assumptions of your chronic condition can make day-to-day working difficult.

Working for yourself allows you to set the rules, the boundaries, and really tailor it around you and your life:

- You get to choose WHEN you work, so it fully fits around your life and needs.
- You can choose WHO you work with, ensuring that you work with like-minded individuals.
- You have full flexibility to take time off for any appointments that you need to attend.
- You build a business that works for YOU and enables you to live a happier life.

I think it is important to note that unfortunately this book is not going to be suitable for everyone who has a chronic condition. Sadly, there are different severities of each chronic condition, and this often differs person to person. For example, with my chronic condition (ME/CFS), it can affect you mildly, moderately or severely. I would put myself in the mild/moderate category as I am mainly housebound, but I can work with lots of pacing and rest.

Running a Business is not for everyone!

Running a *successful* business is not for everyone, and it is certainly not the easy option. Chronic condition or not, certain personality traits or qualities are needed to help to ensure you succeed in running a business.

I have outlined some key traits below. This is not a definitive list, but, in my opinion, these are at the core of every successful business owner.

You need to have a *sense of responsibility*. When you run your own business, the buck stops with you, no one else. You have a lot of responsibilities to juggle, including financial, legal and strategic responsibilities, as well as client responsibilities.

You also need to be able to *risk assess*. As with everything, running your own business comes with an element of risk involved. As a business owner, you need to be able to take calculated risks, which will allow you to make a change and move forward.

To be successful, you need to have *the ability to implement* and be an *action taker*. It is all very well talking about what you want to achieve or writing down what you want to achieve, but it won't happen unless you implement the steps to get there.

You will need to be *self-motivated* and *use your own initiative*. When you run your own business, you do not have a boss there to motivate you or tell you what to do. You are in charge and need to continually keep yourself motivated and moving forward in your business.

I believe that having a *passion for what you do* is essential. If you are *passionate about what you do*, then this will make a huge difference in keeping yourself motivated. If you genuinely love what you do, this will shine through in everything you do and can only have a positive impact on your business.

You need to have *drive and determination* to succeed and be resilient against any challenges that you will encounter along the way. No one likes knock backs, but you need to be able to use these as motivation to adapt and go again.

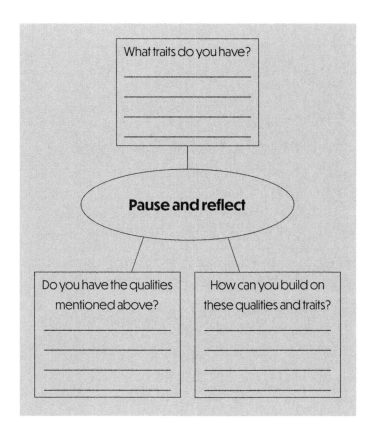

What traits do you have?

_____

_____

_____

_____

Pause and reflect

Do you have the qualities
mentioned above?

_____

_____

_____

_____

How can you build on
these qualities and traits?

_____

_____

_____

_____

How to use this book

Along the way, you will find information, advice and real-life experiences to help you on your way. There are also 'pause and reflect' sections, which include activities for you to work through.

Do you need some help?

If you need some support with the exercises, or want to work through your ideas of running your own business alongside your chronic condition, then why not book a Power Hour with me? We will spend an hour on Zoom together, exploring your ideas, so by the end of the call you have more clarity. To find out more, drop me an email at lisa@thechronicentrepreneur.uk and quote 'The Chronic Entrepreneur' for your 10% discount.

Ready to have a thriving business that works around your chronic condition?

You may be thinking, "Well, yes, I'd love to work for myself, but doing what, exactly?!"

Worry not, I've got you covered!

There are a whole host of things that you can do from home; here are just a few ideas to get you started:

Bookkeeper

Ideal for you if:
- ~ You have a love of numbers.
- ~ You are organised.
- ~ You have high attention to detail.

Nail Technician

Ideal for you if:

~ You are creative.

~ You are able to communicate well with others.

~ You have an eye for detail.

Beauty Therapist

Ideal for you if:

~ You have good people skills.

~ You are able to communicate clearly and sensitively.

~ You have a passion for beauty and self-care.

Hairdresser

Ideal for you if:

~ You have a passion for hair and beauty.

~ You are creative.

~ You have good communication skills.

Virtual Assistant

Ideal for you if:

~ You are organised.

~ You have excellent communication skills.

~ You enjoy supporting others.

Social Media Manager

Ideal for you if:

~ You have a love for social media.

~ You are organised.

~ You are creative.

Marketing Consultant

Ideal for you if:

~ You have a passion for marketing.

~ You have strong communication skills.

~ You have good analytical skills.

Graphic Designer

Ideal for you if:

~ You are creative.

~ You can bring people's vision to life.

~ You can communicate clearly.

Web Designer

Ideal for you if:

~ You have technical skills.

~ You have excellent communication skills.

~ You are creative.

Jewellery Creator

Ideal for you if:

~ You have a good eye for detail.

~ You are organised and can work to a deadline.

~ You are creative.

Crafter

Ideal for you if:

~ You have a passion for making things.

~ You are creative.

~ You are resourceful.

Product Ambassador
Ideal for you if:
- ~ You have a passion for the product.
- ~ You are good at and enjoy networking.
- ~ You have good communication skills.

Personal Trainer
Ideal for you if:
- ~ You are passionate about health and fitness.
- ~ You are able to communicate clearly.
- ~ You enjoy helping others to achieve their goals.

Teacher
Ideal for you if:
- ~ You have a passion for teaching and learning.
- ~ You have strong communication skills.
- ~ You are patient.

Copywriter
Ideal for you if:
- ~ You are excellent at communicating in writing.
- ~ You have good people skills.
- ~ You have an eye for detail.

Author
Ideal for you if:
- ~ You enjoy storytelling.
- ~ You are a good communicator.
- ~ You have good time management skills.

Illustrator

Ideal for you if:

~ You are creative and imaginative.

~ You can bring creative ideas to life.

~ You have excellent attention to detail.

Wedding Planner

Ideal for you if:

~ You are organised and can work to deadlines.

~ You have excellent communication skills.

~ You have good people skills.

Photographer

Ideal for you if:

~ You are creative.

~ You have good communication skills.

~ You have high attention to detail.

Coach

Ideal for you if:

~ You have a passion for helping others.

~ You have good communication skills.

~ You have excellent interpersonal skills.

This list is not exhaustive, but will hopefully help you to see that running your own business really is a possibility across almost all industries. It is important to consider where your skills lie and what you enjoy. Of course, there is always the option of upskilling through courses as well.

Pause and reflect

A simple but effective way of discovering your zone of genius is to:

1. Make a list of ALL the skills that you have; consider past jobs, past opportunities, hobbies, and things you have helped others with.
2. Put a line through anything you do not enjoy.
3. Consider which skills are realistic or manageable for you to do alongside your chronic condition, and put a line through anything that isn't.
4. Also consider which skills are going to be most valuable to potential clients and customers.

Do you need some help?

If you need some support with this exercise, or want to work through your ideas of running your own business alongside your chronic condition, then why not book a Power Hour with me? We will spend an hour on Zoom together, exploring your ideas, so by the end of the call you have more clarity. To find out more, drop me an email at lisa@thechronicentrepreneur.uk and quote 'The Chronic Entrepreneur' for your 10% discount.

Getting Started

Once you've decided what it is you are going to do, the next thing is to start planning what you need to get in place in order to run your own business. Before you get started, it is crucial to get *all* the essentials in place. This will ensure that you are protected, limit any stress and also reflect your professionalism to your clients.

A passion for what you do

One of the most important things is having a passion for what you do. I'm sure we have all worked in jobs where we have hated the tasks that we are carrying out, and you begin to resent the work being asked of you and dreading those Monday mornings.

If you are going to be starting your own business, you really do need to love what you do, you need to have the passion and drive to deliver the very best service to your clients and to take your business from strength to strength.

Running a business is not for everyone, it is hard work and does require ongoing determination and drive. When things become a challenge, you need to be able to remind yourself why you started and how much you love what you do; this will help to ensure that your business is a success and that it doesn't fail at the first stumbling block.

Jen Parker, fellow chronic condition sufferer, of Fuzzy Flamingo echoes this:

> "My best advice is to ensure you are doing something you love and are passionate about. It is really hard work running a business, there is no point in pretending it's not, so you need to be motivated to get up and do it come Monday morning. If it's something you love then that hard work won't feel like a bad thing."

Read more on this aspect in "The importance of your 'why'" chapter starting on page 31.

What's in a name?

One of the key elements of setting up your own business is

giving it a name and establishing the overall brand.

Your business name could be reflective of the type of business you run, it might be a play on words, or it could even be a made-up word.

Consider:

- Is it easy to say?
- Is it easy to spell?
- Does it meet the requirements of HMRC? (These differ depending on what type of business structure you choose to set up.)
- Is it future-proof?
- Are the corresponding website domain name and social media handles available?

The name of your business comes hand in hand with your business brand. Branding is so much more than just a logo, it's almost like the personality of your business. It's your mission, your values, your unique selling points. As potential clients and customers get to know your business brand, they will associate certain thoughts or feelings with it. You need to make sure these are the right associations for your business. You need to be consistent in your messages, and with your branding, including your logo, your business colours, fonts and the language that you use. All of this will feed into whether or not those potentials convert into a client or customer.

Remember that your brand can evolve with time, and you may even find you need a whole rebrand at some point in your business journey, and that is okay. When I started my business, I was Lisa Jane Virtual Assistant and registered as a sole trader. I later swapped to Lisa Porto, as I wanted to move away from the virtual assistant side of things. When I decided to become a limited company, I needed to rethink my business name once more, and I did a lot of work on both my business mission and values, which resulted in Empowered Online Limited being born.

Pause and reflect

1. Make a list of any ideas you have for your new business name. Don't forget to work your way through the consideration questions above too, to help you shortlist the names.
2. Start thinking about your branding.

Register with HMRC

You absolutely must register with HMRC, so that you can pay any tax due and national insurance contributions. At the time of writing, the HMRC recommends you to register as soon as you can after launching your business, but no later than the 5th October of your business's second tax year.

I would advise you to check the government website for the most up to date information:

https://www.gov.uk/set-up-business

The website provides you with information on the whole process, including how to register as a sole trader, limited company or a partnership.

The majority of people set up as a sole trader initially, but I would always recommend you check with your accountant for advice on this and what is best for your situation.

Depending on the nature of your business, you may also be required to have particular licences or permits, so it is always advisable to check with your local council or authority.

Register with ICO

The Information Commissioner Office or ICO regulates data protection within the UK. This is in line with UK GDPR (General Data Protection Regulation), which is the law that regulates privacy and data protection.

If you are an organisation or sole trader who processes personal information of any description, you will need to pay an annual data protection fee to the ICO. There are some exemptions, so I would recommend that you visit their website and complete the assessment: https://ico.org.uk/for-organisations/data-protection-fee/self-assessment/

In reality, if you are processing any type of client personal information you will need to pay a fee. The process is fairly straightforward, all you need to do is visit https://ico.org.uk/for-organisations/data-protection-fee/ and complete the online form along with payment of your fee.

Insurance

Insurance is something that needs to be in place from the very start. Please do not wait for your first client, or not worry about having it in place because you are *only* working with family or friends. Things can go wrong with family and friends too, and the insurance needs to be in place to be able to protect you and your business.

There are several different types of insurance available to help protect you and your business from claims, losses, accidents, damages and fees. Depending on your business, you may need some or all of the following:

- Public Liability
- Product Liability
- Professional Indemnity
- Cyber, data and Security
- Employer's liability
- Legal expenses
- Office

- Directors and Officers
- Occupational personal accident

I would suggest getting in touch with Markel Direct UK for your insurance needs, they provide comprehensive cover and also provide access to their online law hub, which includes a whole range of legal templates and guidance to support your business. Be sure to use my affiliate link https://quote.markeluk.com/referafriend/0120f815-765f-4aa7-8361-9b2bee9ae263

or code (*CD29514*) when getting a quote from them.

Legal Documents

Legal documents such as terms and conditions are also essential for any business. As mentioned previously, it doesn't matter if it's a new client, your sister or a friend, you really do need some type of legal agreement in place between the two of you. This will clearly set both yours and their responsibilities and expectations. It will help to avoid any grey areas and protects you as a business owner, but also them, as your client.

Markel Direct UK, who I mentioned earlier, provides access to their Legal Hub, which consists of a number of legal templates that you can personalise to your business.

Bookkeeping

The HMRC requires all businesses to keep records of their finances. This is to ensure that you complete your tax return with the correct information.

There are no rules on how you need to keep your records if you are self-employed. They can be paper-based, in a spreadsheet or you can use online software such as FreeAgent.

It can be useful to keep your business finances separate from your personal finances. Depending on your business structure, you may or may not need to have a business bank account, but in all cases it does make it easier to do your bookkeeping. I use Starling Bank for my own business banking and would highly recommend them. If you join Starling Bank and open an account, they'll plant a tree for us. Just use my link to apply for an account: https://www.starlingbank.com/referral?code=hZ2IxL.

It is always sensible to plan ahead for any tax due and national insurance contributions. At the time of writing this book, my bookkeeper recommends putting 30% of your profit away for tax and national insurance.

Boundaries

Boundaries are an important part of running a business, especially when doing so from home, but it is also something that evolves in time. I would say that it is useful to be aware of boundaries and maybe consider what your boundaries are or what you want them to be. I would just bear in mind that your boundaries might not come into play immediately as there might be certain situations that trigger you to reaffirm them.

I'll give you an example: I began working with a new client, and within the first few days of working together I received several emails, phone calls and WhatsApp messages about the same query, all within minutes of each other. As you can imagine, this made me feel overwhelmed and under pressure, even though the query she was asking wasn't urgent. I contacted her and explained that I would always get back to her, always within forty-eight hours but usually lots sooner. I also asked her to contact me on one communication channel, preferably email, as text messages tend to get lost. Going forward we were both on the same page and both clear on the boundaries.

Something that works quite well is to have an auto-responder on your emails that thanks them for their email and lets them know when you will be back in touch, plus any other useful information such as how to book a call with you. An example of this is:

Thanks so much for getting in touch.

I only check my inbox twice a day and will be touch with you within the next 48 hours.

If you are interested in working together, you can book your free 20-minute consultation here.

You may also find it useful to visit my website.

As well as having clear boundaries with your clients, you also need to have these with friends, family and others who may live in the same household. For some reason, some people seem to think that because you are working at home, you are not busy! As a people pleaser, this is something I've found difficult, but a wise woman once reminded me that time is money, and that unlike in an employed position, when you are self-employed you are not paid for your time off.

More importantly, when you have a chronic condition, it is important to consider the factors that may cause a flare up of your symptoms. As an example, with myself, any interactions with others have an impact on and increases my fatigue. So, if I were to have a few people call in to see me, unplanned, during my working day, this would have an impact on the other tasks planned for the day and may mean they are not completed as expected.

So, there is the financial impact but also the impact on your health and client deadlines too. If you can, I'd recommend getting these types of boundaries in place sooner rather than later.

Somewhere quiet to work

If you are running your own business from home, then you'll need somewhere suitable to work. Depending on the type of work you plan to do, your workspace will require different key elements. For example, a virtual assistant's workspace needs would differ to that of a beauty therapist.

Ideally, your workspace should be quiet and free from distractions. However, as with everything, when you have a chronic condition, you need a degree of flexibility. Some business types will allow more flexibility than others, but it is important to try and find what works best for you.

I have currently got four different places to work in my home, depending on how I am feeling:

- In my office (a converted spare room).
- Outside at the garden table.
- On the sofa.
- In or on my bed.

People without chronic conditions are often surprised about the bottom two. For me, the two main elements I struggle with are widespread pain and debilitating fatigue. Some days I cannot sit and work from my desk and the most comfortable option is on the sofa or bed.

Don't ever feel guilty if you do need to work from bed or the sofa. Remember that it's your business and you are running it for the flexibility to work more comfortably on days that are more challenging.

As long as you can do what you need to in order to serve your clients, then it really doesn't matter where you work from or what others think of this.

Do be mindful that working from bed or the sofa (or anywhere other than a supportive chair/desk set up) can have an impact on your health because of your posture, so it is not a long-term solution. But you will find what works best for you.

Equipment

The equipment that you need for running your own business will differ greatly depending on what the focus of your business is.

Most businesses these days will need a computer, either for communication purposes and/or record keeping. The specification of the computer is likely to differ depending on your business needs. For example, a graphic designer may need a higher spec due to the software they are using. It is important that you purchase the correct computer for your software needs and general usability.

Another consideration, regarding a computer, is whether to have a laptop or desktop. This is a personal preference. When you have a chronic condition, a degree of flexibility is needed, so a laptop may be the preferred option. A printer can also be useful and is essential for some business owners. A comfortable keyboard and mouse (additional supports if helpful) are also useful if you are using them regularly.

If your business is mainly office based then a good desk, supportive chair and the right set-up of these for your personal physicality are recommended to support your health. Good posture while you're working can really benefit your health, as Jen Parker from Fuzzy Flamingo has found:

"Having had an occupational therapist give recommendations to me when I was full-time employed, which couldn't be implemented at the time, I knew a few things that may help me. I invested in a stand-up/sit-down desk with an electric mechanism to raise and lower my desk, giving me the opportunity to work in different positions depending on what is most comfortable at that time. I have found that alternating between standing and sitting, as well as doing stretches or walking to the kitchen once every hour, really helps to reduce my stiffness and pain. I also have a chair with adjustable lumbar support to help my back and a foot rest to ensure I'm sitting in the right position when at my desk. These have been instrumental in keeping me working comfortably."

People often feel they should have a second mobile phone. In my opinion, this isn't essential, but it is nice to have, and allows you to have that line between business and personal. If it is something you feel you would like, or if you will be using the phone a lot for your particular business, then I would recommend seeing if your personal mobile phone has dual sim ability (many do now) and then you could get a pay as you go sim card, which could help to keep costs down.

Pause and reflect

Make a list of all the equipment that you believe you need for your business and consider if it is essential or a bonus. This will help you to prioritise and budget when you are in the early stages of setting up your business.

Professional email address

You may read this one and think, "Well, that's not really essential, it's not going to stop me setting up." No, it won't stop you setting up, but it could influence whether a potential client goes with you over someone else.

Picture the scenario: you need a plumber. Are you more likely to book the plumber with the professional email address, e.g. info@companyname.co.uk, or the one with the hotmail or gmail address? I know which I'd go with, if there wasn't anything else between them.

Setting up a professional email address doesn't have to be expensive. If you have a website, many hosting companies will provide you with an email account specific to your domain name, or alternatively you can use a provider such as Google Workspace (with or without a website). If you are yet to purchase a domain, you can do so by visiting my website https://domains.empowered-online.co.uk/ and contact me for 10% off your first year on either the Google Workspace Business Starter plan or the Google Workspace Business Standard plan.

Once you have a professional email address set up then you'll need to set up your email signature. There are lots out there to choose from, and I would highly recommend having a look at Hubspot's email signature generator.

Website

Having a website is another element that is debated a lot in terms of whether it is really needed when setting up a business. In my opinion, having a website is a must. It demonstrates professionalism and authority of your business, and will help to increase your online presence and visibility.

If you are sitting there shaking your head, and quite content with your social media, then a word of warning. You do not own your social media pages and the platform can delete yours at any time, without warning. Social media is a great way for you to promote your business, however I personally think this needs to be alongside a website.

When you first start out, you do not need an elaborate, multi-page website, a single page will suffice to get started, and the website can grow as your business grows. I offer one-page websites, which are perfect for new businesses. To find out more, drop me an email at lisa@thechronicentrepreneur.uk and quote 'The Chronic Entrepreneur' for your 10% discount.

Reliable internet connection and back-up plan!

Depending on the type of work you are undertaking, you may be dependent on internet access. If this is the case, please make sure that you have a reliable connection and, if you don't, then you need a back-up plan.

I spent some time out in France for the winter season a few years ago and the wi-fi at our apartment was awful. I was working as a virtual assistant at the time and was therefore very dependent on the internet. As a back-up, I had a dongle through my mobile phone provider, and also had a couple of cafes that were local and had good wi-fi. Without these two elements being considered and planned for, working abroad for those five months would have been more disruptive and would have increased my stress levels – never good when you have a chronic condition, as you'll know. With a little forward planning, I was able to make my day-to-day working easier and reduce any potential stress. It also meant no implications on client work that was booked in.

As well as cafes or restaurants, there are also:

- Co-working spaces.
- Going to a friend's home.
- Going to a member of family's home.

With the friend's or family's home, as discussed earlier in this chapter, remember to have clear boundaries in place, if this is somewhere you need to go and work.

If you've not heard of co-working, then in short it is a shared space where there are hot desks available for people to come and work. These types of places often have the option of hiring private office spaces or meeting rooms too. Some co-working spaces are open during office hours only, whereas others are open for hours outside of this. If you search in Google for 'co-working near me', it should bring up some options local to you for you to explore.

The importance of your 'why'

As discussed earlier in the book, your *why* is a crucial part of running a successful business. You need to be clear on this from the start, as it will help you to keep going on the days you feel like you can't. It will also help you with some decision making, in terms of whether what you are needing to decide upon aligns fully with your *why* and isn't going to compromise this at all.

My Story

For me, my *why* is to be able to work flexibly around my chronic condition, have a better quality of life and ultimately be happy.

I was diagnosed with myalgic encephalomyelitis (ME), also known as chronic fatigue syndrome (CFS), back in

July 2018 and additionally suspected fibromyalgia in 2019. These diagnoses followed me being poorly with glandular fever in November 2017, which saw me off sick for a good six weeks from my full-time job as an NVQ assessor. The month prior to becoming poorly, I had actually handed in my notice to take some time out, as the company had been in the midst of lots of restructuring.

After taking some time out from working, I applied for some temporary office work. As someone who had always worked in education, starting out as a teacher and moving into assessing, I knew it wasn't something I could go back to, due to the hours, level of work I'd need to do and the stress it was likely to put on me, so I looked into something that still utilised my skill set but didn't require lots of out-of-hours working.

I was offered some work temping in an office. The job itself was okay, and the managers were very understanding of any appointments I needed to attend, but the long hours (which unfortunately were not negotiable) and commute in and out each day, which could take anything from forty minutes to, at its worst, two hours, was draining. At this point, I should mention I had not had my diagnosis but continued to push through as much as I could, thinking it was just the aftermath following the glandular fever. I was juggling this temp job, as well as a couple of other ad hoc jobs, which I used to love but were becoming a struggle due to having no energy, and spent any other time sleeping.

Later in the year, after my diagnosis, I accompanied my partner Chris to France for the ski season and was unfortunate to be involved in an accident, where I broke my wrist and needed surgery to have a metal plate fitted. I didn't want to spoil the trip for my partner, and I loved being out in the mountains, so we decided to stay. I then had a three-month period where I was out of action, where none of the seasonal jobs would have been suitable with one fully functional wrist. So, I took the opportunity to use this time and to build a business that would work around me. I knew that returning to a full-time job when we were back was not an option, if I wanted to be able to live my best life, despite having this chronic condition.

I can now plan my work around me, rather than the other way around. If I need to go and sleep for a few hours, then I can. I can choose when, what and who I work with. This also helps limit any stress, as when you have chronic condition stress can often make things a whole lot worse. By taking control, I have a better quality of life, and am able to do something that I really love, which, in turn, has a positive impact on myself, as well as those around me. I don't have any desire to return to an employed role, as I know it would have a detrimental effect on me and all the progress I have made so far. It wouldn't give me the flexibility I need, and it would reduce my quality of life and happiness. On tough days, I remind myself of my *why*, why I started and how far I have come. This helps to continue to fuel my drive and determination.

Stories of other warriors

Here a few other examples of amazing entrepreneurs with chronic conditions who have set up and run a successful business, explaining their reasons behind the decision:

"I had lots of problems working a standard nine-to-five in an open-plan office. My chronic condition is treated with immunosuppressants to inhibit my immune system attacking my own body. A side effect of this is I was catching every little bug going round the office and being knocked off my feet for a lot longer than others. This added pressure to my colleagues having to cover for me, increased my stress because of the guilt that came with that and the worry that I could fall ill at any moment, and it became a vicious circle. When I was on maternity leave with my first baby, my health drastically improved with not being in that environment, plus childcare costs would eat up most of my wages, so the decision was made with my husband's and the publishing house's support that I would go freelance. My original intention was that this would be a temporary thing until the kids went to school, when I thought I would get a 'proper job', but it evolved into a business I love and such a better work-life-health balance that I'd never go back to being employed!"

Jen Parker, Fuzzy Flamingo

"I have Addison's disease and a recurring pituitary (base of brain) tumour. The impact is neurosurgery and radiotherapy as and when the tumour grows (four times to date), and with each time comes a longer recovery period and quality of life reduces. Addison's disease is a potentially fatal disease, which means my body cannot cope with any stress, and thus I take medication three times a day to keep me alive. The condition also gives me chronic fatigue. I have had these conditions since 2012 (Addison's 2015). In 2015, I could no longer hold down a nine-to-five with the endless hospital appointments, excessive time off for treatment and the fatigue. Just the twenty-five minute commute to work would be my limit."

Catherine Gladwyn, Catherine Gladwyn Limited

"I'm a virtual assistant and community manager and have been running my own business for nearly four years while suffering from fibromyalgia. I made the decision while on maternity leave from my employed job with my second child. It was mainly due to not wanting to go back to employment but also due to my health, as I remembered how much I struggled to juggle work and a new baby and my health before and didn't want to be putting so much pressure on my body again."

Carole Searle, CS Business Support

"My background is as a chartered accountant and a qualified teacher. I have been running my social enterprise Funancial Training since 2013 and more recently my consultancy. In 2016, I was diagnosed with an autoimmune disease called Graves' disease. I had never heard of it before, and it took approximately three months for partial diagnosis and six for full diagnosis. I lost two stone in about six weeks, had shortness of breath, fatigue, shaking, heat intolerance and foggy brain, to name a few of the symptoms. I had to stop working for six months, but as someone who teaches the importance of money management and investments, I was able to drawdown on my property investment to supplement my income. I was on the verge of depression but saved by the fact that I had to get up every morning to take my son to school, otherwise I would've stayed in bed all day."

Jackie Stewart, Funancial Training and Consultancy Ltd

So, what is your *why?* Don't worry if you have more than one. Your *why* or *whys* will be completely personal to you and your circumstances.

Pause and reflect

Spend some time thinking about your **why**. Take as much time as you need to really dig deep. Once you've identified your **why**, write it down and put it somewhere that you can see it. This will help you to remember why you started on those harder days, and also help you to keep any decisions you make aligned with your **why**, keeping you true to yourself.

Me, Myself and I

Mindset

Your mindset can have a huge impact on how successful your business will be. Your mindset is made up of the perceptions and beliefs you have about yourself. These shape how you approach and react to different situations as well as your confidence and expectations.

According to Carol Dwerk, there are two mindsets: fixed and growth mindsets. A fixed mindset is where you have the belief that everything is set in stone, your intelligence, skills and qualities. Whereas someone with a growth mindset will see the potential in the situation, enjoys a challenge, and knows that they can learn and develop their skills to move closer to achieving their goal. Something else she talks about is how, quite often, those who succeed are those with a growth mindset, rather than that of a fixed mindset, as they are enthusiastic about what they do and are constantly striving to improve themselves.

Mindset can have a bigger impact on things than I think we realise, but there are lots of things you can do to develop this, if it is something that you find is holding you back. Small things like practising daily gratitude and having daily affirmations can really help keep your mindset in a good place.

Fears and worries

It is only natural that you will have some fears and worries when starting your own business. It is not an easy thing to do, let alone when you are managing your chronic condition at the same time.

Some examples of worries people have include:

> "What if I fail? I don't want to not work and go on benefits. I didn't want to let my conditions define me, but working for others was becoming an option that was no longer viable."
>
> *Catherine Gladwyn*

> "Worries of not having a regular paycheck, so I kept my job in the city for a few years but reduced my

hours so I could build up my business until I could go full time."

Jackie Stewart

"Will I be able to cope with all the demands of running my own business and coping with fibromyalgia?"

Carole Searle

"Huge worries! I knew nothing about running a business, there were massive gaps in my knowledge, and it was a scary prospect that I would be doing it on my own."

Jen Parker

You might have a long list of fears and worries, some may be similar to the examples above, some will be different as they will be personal to you and your situation. The important thing to remember is that it is perfectly normal to have these worries. Quite often you can reflect on these concerns and look at how they can be overcome.

Pause and reflect

If you feel that you have lots of fears and worries swimming around your head, then work through the following questions:

1. What are your worries? (Consider writing these down,

as sometimes it can help just getting the thoughts out of
your head and on to paper.)

2. How likely they are to happen? (Rationalising your
    thoughts and putting them into perspective can
    sometimes help.)

3. What could you put in place to prevent it from
    happening?

When imposter syndrome strikes...

A big thing that causes worry is something often referred to
as *imposter syndrome*, where you might not think you are not
good enough to be running your own business, think you
are not worthy of what you are charging, and just generally
doubt your abilities and feel like you are something of a
fraud. You can experience imposter syndrome at any time
in your business journey. I think it's often worse when you
have a chronic condition as well, as it throws in other doubts.

There are things you can do to manage when imposter
syndrome strikes:

*   Acknowledge how you are feeling and be kind to
    yourself. (This is where those positive affirmations
    really come into play!) Is how you are talking to yourself
    how you would talk to a friend? If the answer is no,
    then you need to try and improve the self-talk and not
    be so hard on yourself.

- Surround yourself with supportive people. You need people around you who are cheering you on to succeed. As someone with a chronic condition, I'm sure you know the impact and importance of those around you, and the same goes for business. If you have the wrong people around you, it will have a detrimental effect. I developed a supportive network, one that supports and cheerleads one another. I also have a couple of business besties who are always there for me when I am having a wobble or to share my achievements with – and I wouldn't be without them!

- Keep track of your achievements and reflect on your journey to see how far you have come. This one is really important but often something that is missed. It is really easy to just keep going, but if you never pause and take stock then you will never see how far you have come. You could do this in a number of ways: keep a list in a notebook or on a document on the computer. You could even have a notice board to add any achievements and anything else meaningful to.

- Try not to compare yourself to other business owners. This is really hard, but it can have a really negative effect. You need to try and remember that even if you are running a business offering similar services to another business owner, both will be different, as you are both individual and will put your unique touch on your endeavours. This is what will set you apart from one another and to your clients.

TOP TIP: If you are finding that you are getting triggered by another business owners' posts on social media then why not just hide their posts, so you don't see them? This is something I have done, on more than one occasion, and although it may sound silly to some, it has actually really helped me to focus on me and my business, rather than them.

You can't pour from an empty cup...

Self-care is hugely important when you are managing a chronic condition or running a business. When you are managing both a chronic condition and a business, self-care is essential and non-negotiable in ensuring you can achieve what you set out to do.

Put simply, self-care is taking care of yourself. It's actively caring for yourself in a way that maintains or improves your health and well-being, physically, mentally and emotionally.

Self-care will look slightly different for everyone. After all, we are all unique and have individual needs. Essentially, self-care will be made up of things you can do or choose not to do, which will make you feel better in mind, body and spirit. It can involve a number of elements, helping you to reduce stress (something that can heighten the symptoms of your chronic condition) and reduce burnout. Self-care is probably one of the biggest factors in enabling chronically ill people to run, manage and grow their own businesses.

Jackie Stewart, a chronic condition sufferer, recognises the need to listen to her body:

> "I have now put things in place so I don't add more stress to my life worrying that when I can't work, I can't earn. I no longer feel guilty for taking time out when I need to rest, my condition alerts me to when I am doing too much, and I listen and rest."

Something I would highly recommend is having a self-care toolkit. Something that you can refer to, to ensure you practice self-care, maintain your boundaries and keep stress to a minimum. This could be a list on your phone, a notebook, a box of items. There is no definitive way it should be or look, it is personal to you. You can then refer to this as needed, but also plan to include aspects from this daily, as part of your routine.

My self-care toolkit is made up of a number of elements, and it is something that is continually evolving, being tweaked and added to. Some of the elements include:

- A journal where I practise daily gratitude, choose a maximum of three things to focus on for the day, celebrate my wins, track my habits and reflect on the day.

- I have a list of boundaries that I try to work to. For example, I limit the number of calls I have in a day and only have calls on certain days of the week.
- A box with notes, cards, photos and keepsakes from my nearest and dearest. If I am having a down day, this is guaranteed to make me feel a little better.
- A weighted blanket (and several other tactile blankets around the house), which I use daily.
- A heat pad, fingerless gloves and pain meds to help manage my pains.
- I go outside daily for some fresh air, even if it is just out in the garden for half an hour.

Pause and reflect

1. Do you practise self-care?
2. How do you take care of yourself?
3. Are there any additional things you could be doing to take better care of yourself?

Need some help with this? Drop me an email at lisa@ thechronicentrepreneur.uk and I'll send you my free Self-Care Toolkit Guide, which gives you some ideas of things you could include.

Managing Expectations

Expectations is something that is essential when it comes to running a business. However, when you have a chronic condition too it is even more so. It is something that is part of your self-care. You are essentially protecting or shielding yourself; ensuring you reduce stress and overwhelm, which is important for any business owner but particularly one also managing a chronic condition. You need to manage the expectations of yourself and others, including clients, associates and even friends and family.

The acceptance of your chronic condition comes into play when we talk about expectations. I guess it's being honest with yourself, even when it's not easy to hear, that sadly you can't do everything, but that this is okay and what you do, you do well. Your chronic condition does not make you any less of a person, it just means you need to adapt. I know this is easier said than done, and some days you may be okay with this and other days you won't. I have days where I am okay with adapting, but other days I get frustrated, as well as a whole host of other emotions. It is okay to feel like this and it's just part of the day-to-day living with a chronic condition.

> "Don't forget you're human. It's okay to have a meltdown, just don't unpack and live there. Cry it out and then refocus on where you are headed."
>
> **Unknown**

Something to consider and that can actually help with expectations is disclosing your chronic condition to your clients. This is a personal preference and something you need to be comfortable with, and possibly links to how accepting you are of your condition. When I first started my business, I kept my chronic condition to myself, but as I became more confident within my business and more accepting of my condition, I have started to disclose this more with clients. Quite often it might come up in conversation, when talking about my working hours, or turnaround times for projects. Someone once asked me if I was worried about putting off potential clients. My answer was simple: no, it didn't worry me. My chronic condition is part of me, but it doesn't define me, so I don't really want to work with people who are going to judge me on having a chronic condition. This is another plus of running your own business – you can choose who you do and do not work with.

As someone who is a people pleaser, and doesn't like to say no to anything, I used to find myself saying yes to things that I either didn't want to do or hadn't got capacity to do. I had to remind myself that firstly I didn't choose to run my own business to carry out tasks I didn't enjoy, and that I have a chronic condition. If I take on work I haven't got the capacity to do (this includes carrying out work at times you should be resting), then all I'm going to do is overwhelm myself, and potentially miss client deadlines, both of which will lead to more stress and a flare in your symptoms.

When it comes to clients, always under-promise, and over-deliver. This will help to protect you, your time and ensure you deliver a project or task on time.

If you find yourself saying yes to things all the time and it is having a knock-on effect on your health and well-being, then there are a few things that will help:

- Give yourself time before saying yes (or no). Say something like, "Let me check my diary and I'll come back to you on this." This will give you time then to reflect on what you've been asked and to ask yourself three questions:
  ~ Have I got the capacity to do this task? (Without having an impact on any other work I have booked in or without sacrificing my own time.)
  ~ Is the task something within my skill set?
  ~ Is the task something I enjoy doing?
  If you answer no to any of these questions, then the task is likely something you need to turn down.

- Identify other ways of saying no. Try to reframe your response from no, to provide other options. For example, rather than saying "no, sorry", say "I can't do the work this week but would Wednesday work for you?" or "Unfortunately this is not something I can help you with". Saying no is okay, and is important to reinforce your boundaries, but it is something than can be said in a range of ways.

- Be clear in your mind how much time you have in your day or week – this will help you to manage the expectation of if you can do that new task or not.

I think it is important to say that managing expectations is not always easy, and if it is something that you find difficult, it will get easier with time. I know for me, as time has gone on, I have slowly got better at managing expectations for myself and others in general.

Pause and reflect

1. Do you have any boundaries in place currently?
2. If yes, review these – are they all still relevant?
3. If no, have a go at identifying some boundaries for yourself and others, thinking about the positive impact having that boundary in place will have. E.g. it will ensure you do not get overwhelmed.

Planning

"A goal without a plan is just a wish."

Antoine de Saint-Exupéry

When you run a business, it's important to have a plan in place, so you know where you are heading, and how you are going to get there.

When things are planned, carefully considered and recorded, they are more likely to happen. A study carried out by Dr Gail Matthews at Dominican University, who had 267 people divided into five groups, found that the group of people who had recorded their goals with a clear plan of action achieved much more than any of the other groups.

There are lots of different planning strategies and planning tools out there. Having a plan in place for your business doesn't need to be a complex task. It often helps to keep things simple and not to over complicate things.

The Foundations

It is important to get clear on the vision, mission and core values of your business. This provides you with clarity of your vision for the future, your mission in terms of the service/products you wish to provide and the problems it will solve for your clients, the values you wish to uphold, and the type of clients you wish to work with.

The following questions will help you to focus on the core aspects of your business:

- What is your business vision? (Think of this in terms of how it looks for you and your clients/customers.)
- What are your core values?
- Who is your ideal customer or client?
- What challenges do they have?
- How will your products or services solve the problem(s)?
- How will you deliver these products or services?
- How will what you offer or deliver stand out over others? What makes you unique?
- What do you *need* to earn?
- What would you *love* to earn?
- How much will you charge?

Keep this document in whatever format works best for you, and remember it is a working document that can be amended and tweaked at any time. Any planning documents should be working documents, as a degree of flexibility is needed, especially when you have a chronic condition.

Pause and reflect

Spend some time working through the questions in this section to get your foundations finalised.

Goal Setting

Once you have your foundations in place, you can look at setting yourself some goals, which will help you to get where you want to be.

One way of doing this is to work backwards from your business vision. Consider what you want to achieve in the long-term and then work out what you need to do to get there. If you set yourself an income target for five years' time, then you might want to look at what that means annually, year by year and then maybe monthly over the next year. You can look at what you need to do each month to hit this income goal. For example, it might be you need 'X number of clients', or to sell 'X number of products or services'. You can then think about what you need to do to help you achieve this. For example, posting on your social media five times a week, building an audience via your email list, etc. You are essentially breaking your big dreams and aspirations into smaller, bitesize steps.

Back in my teaching days, when I planned lessons, I made sure my lesson objectives were SMART:

- **S**pecific.
- **M**easurable.
- **A**chievable.
- **R**ealistic.
- **T**imebound.

This model ensured that I was clear on what I was teaching and what I wanted the children in my class to learn from the lesson. Due to the objective being so clear, it then made assessing the children's progress really straightforward. The SMART model can be applied to any type of objective, aim or goal. Using the SMART model, you can write goals that are clear and more likely to be met. Think about it, if you have a goal that is quite vague and open-ended, it is going to be harder to achieve it or to review the progress that you have made towards it. Here is an example:

An example of a goal that *isn't* SMART:
To earn an additional £1000

An example of a SMART goal:
To earn an additional £1000, by selling 10 power hour sessions in the month of June.

I would highly recommend displaying these goals where you can see them, to remind yourself of what you are striving to achieve as well as reviewing them regularly.

You can set goals of different terms: short, medium and long-term. Just remember to allow yourself a degree of flexibility; planning with your chronic condition in mind.

Remember, as well, to celebrate your achievements. These could include achieving a goal or working towards a goal. *Both are steps forward.*

Pause and reflect

Identify one long-term goal and one short-term goal and write it out following the SMART framework.

Day-to-day Planning

I used to squeeze as much as possible into my day, neglecting my self-care, saying yes to everyone, because I was afraid of letting people down, and have run myself into the ground on more than one occasion. I have learnt the hard way that this is not sustainable for anyone, even less so when you have a chronic condition. More importantly, I have learnt that it doesn't have to be like this. It just requires a little bit of day-to-day planning, but planning that is flexible and works for you when you have a chronic condition.

It is important to take into consideration your boundaries with your day-to-day planning, as it is in my experience that when these are not in place or upheld, things tend to go to pot. Getting clear on your boundaries will really help your day-to-day planning.

Key things to consider with this planning process are:

- The days and hours you plan to work (depending on your work, you may have flexibility with these).
- Business admin.
- The tasks to be carried out.
- Your rest times (for example: time for a nap or a lie down).
- Your breaks (for example: lunch).
- Potential catch-up time (which we will talk more about later).

There may be other elements, too, depending on your individual needs and line of work, but these are a good place to start.

So, what does this look like in practice? For me, it looks a bit like this:

- My core hours are 10am – 3pm Monday to Thursday.
- I have time planned each week to work on my business tasks, and also have a day a month where I focus on my business only (rather than client work).
- I have a morning routine, where I fill in my journal. I don't have a set time for this as it depends very much on how I am feeling, but this is what I do before anything else.
- As part of my journaling, I outline the three tasks I will be working on, and focus on these only.
- I have calls with clients, and I limit these to only one call a day, Tuesday – Thursday (I enjoy my calls with clients, but they have a big impact on my fatigue and I have found this to be a good way of managing this).
- I have a lie down each day.
- I have regular tea breaks and a lunch break. (I pretty much run on tea!)
- My catch-up time is outside of the 10am – 3pm time, but I try where possible to make sure I switch off my laptop by 8pm.

This may seem a little vague, but it gives me the flexibility I need. So, for example, if I need to sleep for a couple of hours then I will and then I make up any time (or the task that needs completing) in my catch-up time.

I also use tools to help me implement this, such as a timer, blocking time in my online calendar, Asana – a project management tool – and a notepad and pen. I have experimented with lots of different systems, and this is what is currently working best for me. You may find that you'd prefer to have everything in a notebook or diary. The best thing to do is try out some tools and see what suits your situation and ways of working best.

Pause and reflect

1. Plan out your perfect week, taking into consideration your line of work and your health.
2. Remember that this is not set in stone. It is important to reflect on how things are going and if things need to change.

How to manage the bad days

When you have a chronic condition, unfortunately bad days and flare ups are inevitable.

So, what do you do?

This is where some of the elements we have discussed earlier in this chapter and other chapters will come into action:

1. Make sure you are as comfortable as you can be – can you work away from your desk today?

2. Is there anything you can do from your self-care toolkit that will help to improve how you are feeling and reduce any symptoms?

3. Review your tasks – what absolutely needs to be done today? If it can be left until tomorrow, then move it to tomorrow. If you have something that needs to be done, see if you can do this in your catch-up time, as if you rest now, you may feel a little better later on in the day.

4. If you work with a team, then see if someone appropriate can assist you.

5. Worst-case scenario, if it is a really bad flare up, then take the day off. As you'll know, if we continue to push through, this can have a negative impact on our existing conditions, making things worse in the long-term. Remember to communicate with any clients/customers as needed. Communication is key and will help to maintain those good relationships.

Pause and reflect

1. Reflect on your bad days and flare ups.
2. Consider: What are they like? How do you manage? What do you need?
3. Implement a back-up plan in advance for these days.

Sales and marketing

You can have the most fantastic business idea, but if you don't tell anyone about it, then no one will know about it, and you are unlikely to make the sales you want or need. Being an introvert, marketing has always been an area in which I have had to push myself. It may not come naturally to some, but it really is an essential part of your business.

Marketing allows you to build your reputation and authority within your area and niche. Your ideal client can get to know you through your website content, blog posts, social media posts and email marketing. People buy from people, and will mostly need to get to know, like and trust you before engaging in your product or service. So don't be afraid to show your personality within your marketing.

In order to appeal to your ideal client, you need to be really clear on who they are, the problems they have and how your products or services will solve these problems. It needs to be all about them, and how your product or service is going to help them to get where they want to be. This process is crucial because without it your messaging within your marketing will not be right, and it won't attract your ideal clients. There is a saying:

> "When you speak to everyone, you speak to no one."
>
> **Meredith Hill**

Plus, it can become very overwhelming, which needs to be avoided at all costs when you have a chronic condition.

Get Visible

There are a number of ways you can get yourself and your business visible:

- Online business directories
  - ~ Online business directories such as Google My Business, Yell.com, Bing Places, Yelp, to name just a few, often allow you to list your business for free. This is a great way of getting your business out there and will also help with Search Engine Optimisation, as long as the information is consistent between the platforms.

~ **TOP TIP:** Review and update all of your listings every six months or so.

- Website
  - ~ In my opinion, as mentioned earlier, a website is a must for your business to showcase your products and services and enhance your professionalism. A website will also help your ideal clients and customers find you, as it helps to increase your online presence and visibility.
  - ~ Having a blog on your website is a great way to get visible as well as demonstrating your knowledge and expertise within your field. It also helps with SEO by keeping your website active.
  - ~ Remember, when you first start out, you do not need an elaborate, multi-page website, a single page will suffice to get started and the website can grow as your business grows. I offer one-page websites, which are perfect for new businesses. To find out more drop me an email at lisa@thechronicentrepreneur.uk and quote 'The Chronic Entrepreneur' for your 10% discount.
- Social Media
  - ~ There are lots of different platforms out there in terms of social media. I would recommend considering which platforms are mostly used by your ideal clients/customers and start with these, so you are putting your energy into the most relevant ones. You can also start with one or two and build on this over time. The one big thing I have learnt is

that it is the consistency that is important, not the number of platforms that you are on. Start small and be consistent. This will help keep social media manageable for you too.
~ **TOP TIP:** Don't solely rely on social media to communicate with and build your audience; you don't own the platform.
• Email Marketing
~ This is a great way to communicate and build an audience, as you have complete control. This includes being able to segment your audience to ensure all content is relevant and of interest to them.

Batch and schedule

As a small business owner or entrepreneur, you will have a lot of different areas of your business to manage. As a small business owner or entrepreneur with a chronic condition, your time is even more precious, especially if, like me, your condition can fluctuate day-to-day or even hour-to-hour. Therefore, I would highly recommend where possible batching your content creation and scheduling posts in advance. So, for example, you could have a day each month where you do your social media and blogs for the month ahead and then another day each month to do the scheduling.

You can also reuse and recycle social media posts, as not everyone will see them the first time. I do this and over time have developed a bank of content. For example, any testimonials are added to my content bank and get posted on one day each week. I also have tips I share in relation to my niche, These again can be reposted over a period of time. I still post fresh content too, but using my content bank helps to take away the overwhelm, and helps me to stay visible on days I find it more difficult.

Systems and automation

Utilising systems and automation helps things run more smoothly, and can provide your customers and clients a better experience. However, when you choose the right systems and automation, it also makes things much easier for you:

- Keeping you organised and on top of things.
- Allowing you to continue to show up, even on those bad days.
- Freeing up time for you to rest and practise self-care.

Within my business, I use a variety of tools and systems, which cover the following key areas of day-to-day operations, customer management, sales and marketing processes, finance, HR and legal. I also automate processes wherever I can, which plays a big part in managing my business day-to-day, alongside my chronic condition.

Day-to-day operations

I use **Asana – a project management tool,** which helps me organise all of my projects, sharing and communicating projects with clients and team members. Each client has their own area, and I manage my workload from here, as I can see exactly what is going on. It's like a digital to do list, and you can also utilise the board view too, which is a bit like using digital Post-it notes. (And who doesn't love a Post-it note?!)

TOP TIP: Be sure to add your working hours in Asana so that you do not get notifications outside of your hours. This will help you to avoid overwhelm and manage stress.

I have **standard operating procedures (SOPs)** in place, which include notes, videos and screenshots. These are also stored on Asana, so it makes it easy to share.

I have a **journal** that I use to structure my weeks and individual days, practising gratitude and also managing my top three tasks.

I love stationery and have several notebooks for different aspects, but one that is particularly useful is the one I use for my client calls. This means all my notes for client calls are in one place, dated with actions highlighted, so I know what I need to do in terms of following up.

I use **Google Workspace** to manage all my files, calendar and emails, and have an auto-responder set up to manage people's expectations of when to expect a response.

It is also great for collaborating on documents and files. If you would like to sign up and are interested in receiving 10% off per user for the first year as a Google Workspace customer, then please use my affiliate link **https://referworkspace. app.goo.gl/oNR8** but also email me and I will send you a discount code. Please note that you must enter your code during your trial sign-up before you check out.

Customer Management

A customer relationship management (CRM) system is important for you to manage your clients efficiently and to track your leads. You can do this in a number of ways, using software or even a spreadsheet.

In my business I use **Dubsado** mainly for this, which is a business management solution. I have mine set up so that my clients are nurtured from the off, and it helps me to capture all the relevant details to manage my leads and conversions. It also helps take the pressure off me to respond manually, as I have automation set up, and have also set up prompts to remind me to do things that need to be done manually. Dubsado offers a free trial for up to three clients, so you can give it a good test run prior to signing up to a paid plan. You can use my affiliate code *empoweredonline* or direct link **dubsado.com/?c=empoweredonline** to receive a discount off your first month or year.

I also use **Asana** to manage my clients too, whereby I set them up a private area for us to collaborate on the tasks.

Sales and marketing process

In order to run a successful business, it is crucial that you know where the next lead is coming from. Referrals are great but this is not sustainable or guaranteed. Being clear on your sales process will help you to ensure you know where your next lead is coming from and reduce stress.

As discussed in an earlier chapter, marketing ensures you get yourself and your business in front of your ideal clients, but you need a way of doing this, a strategy. You essentially want to think about the journey your potential clients will go through to become a client. This is your sales funnel. Consider how you will make potential clients aware of you and your business, what their pain points are and how you can demonstrate that you can help to solve these. So, when they make the decision to buy, they consider you over and above others. Perhaps think about which social media platforms you plan to use, and how many posts you will commit to each week. It might be creating a freebie for your clients to grow your audience and then committing to sending an email out every week to nurture them and keep them up to date.

To make this process easier, I would highly recommend using a scheduling tool such as **ContentStudio** or **MeetEdgar**. Not only does it allow you to schedule posts in advance, you can also add library categories, which allow you to reuse the content too. Both of these features are so useful when you are running your own business, but when you have an unpredictable chronic condition, it really is a godsend, as you can utilise your good days to batch content and get ahead. Something else I do is keep a bank of content in a Google Sheet, which includes all my content that can be reused.

Another thing to consider is an email marketing platform. There are lots out there that you can use, some such as **Mailerlite** or **Mailchimp** are free for a certain number of subscribers, which when you are starting out in business can be a good starting point.

Finance

You will need some sort of system for your finances, be that a spreadsheet or an actual piece of software. If you plan on using a piece of software, **Freeagent** is really user friendly, and at the time of writing this book some banks actually provide it free with your banking. When I first started out, I did my own bookkeeping and tax return, however I now have a fantastic bookkeeper and accountant who manage this for me. If you are going to manage this yourself, I would recommend trying to do your bookkeeping regularly, for example monthly, to enable you to keep on top of it all, and for it not to get overwhelming.

As you start to get busier, too, you can use other applications such as **AutoEntry**, which captures the information from your business bills and then, after categorising them, you can send them to your accounting software. This means you do not have to add everything manually, saving you lots of time.

I use **Starling Bank** for my business banking and found them to be very helpful. The process of setting up was very easy, especially as I could do everything from my phone at home, with no need to visit a bank in person.

HR and legal

As discussed in the *Getting Started* chapter, you'll also need to consider the legal side of things and have appropriate policies and procedures in place according to the type of business that you run.

Pause and reflect

Reflect on the different areas of your business and consider what systems you need to put in place and make a plan of how to do this. If you already have these in place, then why not review these to see if there is anything you could improve.

Finding your tribe

Running your own business can be lonely, and it is therefore important you build up a network of the right type of people, those who share the same work ethic and values as you, to support you. When you have a chronic condition, you need this support network even more. Managing a chronic condition can be a full-time job in itself some days, so if you are running a business too, you will need that support.

> "The biggest lesson has been that I don't have to do it all alone. A support network is so important, and networking has allowed me to find my tribe, my cheerleaders, my peers."
> **Jen Parker**

Surrounding yourself with the right people

In business, and life in general, it is crucial to surround yourself with the right people. What I mean by that is you need supportive people, who are in your corner and cheering you on. This is no different with a chronic condition; you need people who are there for you.

> "We are the average of the five people we spend the most time with."
>
> **Jim Rohn**

As Rohn says in his quote above, the five people we spend the most time with are going to have a big influence on us. When you spend lots of time with certain people, it is only natural that you will pick up on some of their traits, and them yours.

I am lucky to have built up some great relationships with fellow business owners, two in particular I speak to weekly, if not daily, and they are always there in my corner, and me in theirs, cheering each other on.

You are likely to get to know other business owners as your journey in business progresses, and this can be really handy as you grow your business and may need to look to outsource certain parts of it.

You could attend in-person networking events. I'm not a huge fan of these, but they can work well for some people and businesses. Depending on your chronic condition, you may or may not find these easy to attend, so online networking could be a better bet.

Using social media to network can be quite effective, such as Facebook groups, however there is a lot of noise out there, and it is easy to get overwhelmed with these. I think the one thing to say about the Facebook groups is that be choosy with which ones you join. Just because they are free doesn't mean they will provide you with value or be supportive, so be sure to do your homework!

Non-business support

This may seem obvious, but make sure you are getting the support you need to be able to manage your chronic condition. This might be through your GP and medical appointments or even being part of a support forum or a community. It also includes you making time to practise self-care. Remember what we said earlier about needing to look after yourself, so you have more to give. If you are not sure of the support options available, I would suggest talking to your GP and looking at some of the charities out there supporting chronic conditions. You'll find specific ones such as The ME Association and also more generalised ones for chronic condition or pain in general. They will have a range of information and resources for you to access. There is also a number of social media groups, which you can join for free, just be mindful of joining the groups right for you.

Pause and reflect

1. Reflect on the people you spend the most time with and identify your 5 people.
2. What are the positive impact these people have on you?
3. If the impact is not positive, what could be changed to improve this?

Resources

Asana – an online project management tool that allows me to keep on top of all of my work commitments. Desktop and mobile apps are available, making it easier to use on the go.

Google Workspace – to manage all my files, calendar and emails. If you would like to sign up and are interested in receiving 10% off per user for the first year as a Google Workspace customer, then please use my affiliate link **https://referworkspace.app.goo.gl/oNR8** but also email me and I will send you a discount code. Please note that you must enter your code during your trial sign-up before you check out.

FreeAgent – really easy to use and understand accounting software.

Dubsado – a business management solution where I

manage all my clients, questionnaires and contracts. Use **dubsado.com/?c=empoweredonline** for a discount.

ContentStudio – my go to social media scheduler.

Starling Bank – my preferred business bank.

Markel Insurance – business insurance and handy access to their legal documents vault.

Penfold Pensions – easy to manage pensions for self-employed or limited companies alike.

Mailerlite – user friendly email marketing software, that is a great starting point for building your email list, and that will grow with your business.

Final Thoughts

Over the course of this book, I have taken you through the areas I believe to be crucial in setting up a successful business, when you have a chronic condition to manage.

In this final chapter, I have summarised the key steps for you:

- Reflect and evaluate your skillset to help you to identify your perfect business venture
- Get clear on your why – help keep you focussed and keep motivated on the more tricky days
- Get the essentials in place
  - ~ Decide on your business name
  - ~ Establish your branding
  - ~ Register with HMRC
  - ~ Register with ICO
  - ~ Organise any legal documents such as contracts
  - ~ Organise your bookkeeping
  - ~ Identify your workspace

- ~ Identify and purchase any 'must have' equipment
- ~ Purchase a domain name
- ~ Set up a professional email address
- ~ Set up a website
- ~ Have a back up plan
- Remember to continually work on your mindset
- Remember to practice self-care
- Be clear on your boundaries and expectations
- Planning
  - ~ Get the foundations in place
    - What is your business vision? (Think of this in terms of how it looks for you and your clients/customers.)
    - What are your core values?
    - Who is your ideal customer or client? What challenges do they have?
    - How will your products or services solve the problem(s)?
    - How will you deliver these products or services?
    - How will what you offer or deliver stand out over others? What makes you unique?
    - What do you *need* to earn?
    - What would you *love* to earn?
    - How much will you charge?
    - Set realistic and achievable goals
    - Plan your day – with buffer time
    - Have strategies in place to manage your bad days
  - ~ Set yourself achievable goals

- ~ Plan your days, remembering your buffer and rest times
- ~ Plan for your bad days – what strategies can you put in place to support you?
- Sales and Marketing
  - ~ Be crystal clear on who your ideal client is
  - ~ Consider online business directories you could register on
  - ~ Utilise your website
  - ~ Use social media on the platforms your ideal clients will be on
  - ~ Start to build your audience with an email list
- Systems and automations
  - ~ Consider the systems automations which are going to help you to manage your business more efficiently.
- Finding your tribe
  - ~ Consider building connections with other like-minded business owners
  - ~ Consider any non-business support you might need to support you in managing your chronic condition

Do you need some help?

If you need some support with this or you are feeling overwhelmed then why not book a Power Hour with me? We will spend an hour on Zoom together, exploring your ideas, so by the end of the call you have more clarity. To find out more, drop me an email at lisa@thechronicentrepreneur.uk and quote 'The Chronic Entrepreneur' for your 10% discount.

Connect with me online

thechronicentrepreneur.uk

Facebook.com/TheChronicEntrepreneurUK

Instagram.com/TheChronicEntrepreneurUK

linkedin.com/in/LisaPorto

About Lisa

I live in Hertfordshire, UK with my partner Chris and our two cats Freddie and Kiki.

I am a website designer and tech specialist, who works virtually with service-based business owners, particularly coaches and consultants, supporting them to grow their business by simplifying or implementing the techy aspects.

I started my journey as an entrepreneur in early 2010, running a successful photography business for three years as well as a successful business as a nail technician for five years. These ventures were alongside my main job in education, where she worked as a teacher progressing to a tutor and assessor in further and adult education.

In November 2017, I was unfortunate to come down with a bad case of glandular fever, which saw the beginning of things changing in my life. In February 2019, I began my journey in the world of being purely self-employed. This was all following being diagnosed with myalgic encephalomyelitis (ME), also known as chronic fatigue syndrome (CFS), in July 2018 and additionally suspected fibromyalgia in 2019. You can read more about my story in "The importance of your 'why'" chapter starting on page 31.

Since starting my business in 2019 I have:

- replaced and exceed my main employed income
- built a supportive team around me, consisting of an online business manager, a virtual assistant and four associates
- invested in my own personal and professional development
- Transitioned from being self-employed to the director of a limited company – Empowered Online Limited.
- built a business that is flexible and allows me to manage my chronic condition and have a better life overall

I have always been passionate about helping others and wrote this book to inspire and help other people who manage a chronic condition to build a successful business around themselves too, so they can reap the benefits that come with it.

I hope you have enjoyed it, as much as I have enjoyed writing it.

References

18th March 2021

- https://www.entrepreneur.com/article/306578
- https://www.themuse.com/advice/jobs-work-from-home
- https://www.gov.uk/set-up-business
- https://ico.org.uk/

7th August 2021

- https://www.forbes.com/sites/forbescoachescouncil/2019/12/23/13-essential-skills-and-traits-of-successful-business-owners/
- https://www.thebusinesswomanmedia.com/10-personality-traits-need-start-business/
- https://www.gilroygannon.com/14-common-characteristics-of-successful-small-business-owners/

30th August

- https://www.forbes.com/sites/biancamillercole/2020/06/09/5-tips-for-building-a-business-and-a-career-with-chronic-illness-memyalgic-encephalomyelitis/?sh=44e907876f1e
- https://www.business.com/articles/managing-business-with-chronic-illness/
- https://www.blacksburgbelle.com/2016/03/running-a-business-with-chronic-illness/
- https://thesimplifiers.com/podcast/nikita-williams-chronic-illness
- https://onestepoutside.com/prioritising-your-wellbeing-entrepreneur/
- https://craftindustryalliance.org/the-challenges-of-managing-a-craft-business-and-a-chronic-illness/
- https://positivepsychology.com/goal-setting-psychology/

Dweck, Dr Carol, *Mindset* (2017) Robinson: London

Printed in Great Britain
by Amazon

79247498R00058